Curries From The South

By
Aroona Reejhsinghani

V&S PUBLISHERS

Published by:

V&S PUBLISHERS

F-2/16, Ansari Road, Daryaganj, New Delhi-110002
☎ 011-23240026, 011-23240027 • *Fax* 011-23240028
Email info@vspublishers.com • *Website* www.vspublishers.com

Regional Office Hyderabad
5-1-707/1, Brij Bhawan (Beside Central Bank of India Lane)
Bank Street, Koti, Hyderabad - 500 095
☎ 040-24737290
E-mail vspublishershyd@gmail.com

Branch Office Mumbai
Jaywant Industrial Estate, 2nd Floor–222, Tardeo Road
Opposite Sobo Central Mall, Mumbai – 400 034
☎ 022-23510736
E-mail: vspublishersmum@gmail.com

Follow us on:

All books available at **www.vspublishers.com**

© **Copyright:** V&S PUBLISHERS
Edition 2017

CONTENTS

INTRODUCTION

India is famous for its curries. In fact, it is the home of an endless variety of curries, each better than the other. Indians relish hundreds of curries made with vegetables, meat, fish, prawn and eggs. Every zone in India has its own special way of preparing curries, therefore, each curry has a unique flavour. For example, in Southern India, curries are made with coconut, as their base. And in Kerala where coconut grows in abundance, coconut oil is also used for cooking. Bengal specializes in fish curries prepared in mustard oil. In Punjab, which is greatly influenced by Mughal cuisine, one comes across many exotic curries prepared with onion and tomatoes as a base. In Punjabi curries, coconut is rarely used. Curries are always served with plain fluffy boiled rice and papads which are either fried or roasted.

In India, majority of the people are vegetarian, hence there is a greater variety of delicious vegetarian curries prepared with dals and a variety of vegetables, curds and buttermilk. But this does not mean that there is very little to choose in case of non-vegetarian curries. Indian meat curries, in fact, take many forms. Like kofta curries, ground meat is shaped into balls and cooked in a deliciously rich sauce or curry. Then, there are korma curries — spicy and delicious, keema curries — which is ground meat cooked with peas and decorated with hard-boiled eggs.

In this book, I have chosen for you a wide variety of flavours — some simple, some exotic, some extraordinarily delicious. This book contains recipes for some special curries made and enjoyed in South Zone of India. The aim is to make people relish curries of a particular region even if they don't belong to that region. Even the foreigners can try these recipes to relish a unique taste. Here for you is a distinctive selection of curries which are as distinctive as different wines in different bottles.

Aroona Reejhsinghani
502 B, Lila Apts.
opp. Gul Mohar Gardens,
Yari Road, Versova
Bombay-61
Ph – 6360224

1

CURRIES OF ANDHRA PRADESH

Andhra Pradesh is the largest amongst the South Indian states. It is the largest producer of rice in India, therefore people here are very fond of rice. Andhra is also the home of chillies, both green and red varieties. Therefore, it is normal for Andhra people to use chillies liberally in their food. Besides chillies, their curries have few other spices. Hyderabad, which is Andhra Pradesh's capital, has very different cuisine. Since this city was under Muslim rule, the curries popular here have a moghlai influence. These curries are not only delicious in taste but also look nice and tempt one to have a go at them.

VEGETARIAN CURRIES
COCONUT KOFTA CURRY

Ingredients (Serves 8)

For Curry

- 500 grams tomatoes, grated
- 1 tblsp. poppy seeds
- 4 cloves, 4 cardamoms
- 1-inch piece of cinnamon
- 1/4 dry coconut
- 4 red chillies, 6 flakes of garlic
- 1-inch piece of ginger
- 1/2 tsp. turmeric powder
- 1 big onion, minced
- Handful of sliced coriander leaves
- 12 fried cashewnuts
- Salt to taste

For Koftas

- 1 big coconut
- 3 tblsps. gramflour
- 8 green chillies, minced
- 1 large bunch of coriander leaves, minced
- A big handful of mint leaves, minced
- 1 medium onion, grated
- 1/2 tblsp. each of ginger and garlic paste
- 4 ground red chillies
- 1 tsp. garam masala
- Salt to taste

Preparation

Grind the coconut coarsely and mix it and all the kofta ingredients. Form the mixture into round balls and deep fry to a golden colour. Grind all the whole spices, coconut, ginger and garlic to a paste. Heat 3 tblsps. oil and fry onions and ground paste together till the oil comes out. Add tomatoes, salt and turmeric. Cook till tomatoes turn soft, then put in 1 glass of water, bring the mixture to a boil and keep boiling for 5 minutes. Then add koftas and boil for a few more minutes. Decorate with cashewnuts and coriander leaves.

Sweet Potato Curry

Ingredients (Serves 4)

- 250 grams sweet potatoes, boiled and sliced.
- 1 medium onion, minced
- 3 green chillies, minced
- 2 big tomatoes, grated
- 1/4 tsp. turmeric powder
- 1/2 coconut, grated
- 1 tsp. cumin seeds
- 1 tblsp. coriander seeds
- 3 flakes of garlic
- A few curry leaves
- 4 red chillies
- Handful of sliced coriander leaves
- Salt to taste

Preparation

Grind coconut, red chillies, garlic, cumin and coriander seeds to a fine paste. Heat 2 tblsps. oil and fry the onions and green chillies till soft. Add tomatoes and spices and cook. When the oil comes out, add sliced sweet potatoes and ground paste. Put in 2 cups of water along with the remaining ingredients. Cook till the curry turns a little thick. Serve hot.

CHILLI CURRY

Ingredients (Serves 4)

- 24 thick and large green chillies, slit
- 1 tsp. each of ginger and garlic paste
- 2 tblsps. sesame seeds or til
- 25 raw groundnuts
- 1 tsp. cumin seeds, 1 tblsp. coriander seeds
- 1 lime-sized ball of tamarind
- 2 medium onions
- 1/4 tsp. turmeric powder
- Salt and chilli powder to taste

Preparation

Roast til, cumin and coriander seeds and powder them. Grind groundnuts coarsely. Cover tamarind with 2 cups of hot water for 5 minutes and then squeeze out pulp. Heat 2 tblsps. oil and fry onion paste to a light golden colour. Then add groundnuts and powdered spices and fry nicely. Put in the chillies and fry till they start turning brown. Pour in tamarind and cook till the gravy turns a little thick.

COCUM KADI

Ingredients (Serves 2)

- 250 grams lady's fingers, sliced
- 12 cocums
- 3 green chillies, slit
- 1/2 coconut
- 1 medium onion, grated
- 1/2 tsp. each of ginger and garlic paste
- A few curry leaves
- Handful of coriander leaves
- 1/4 tsp. turmeric powder
- Salt and chilli powder to taste

Preparation

Fry lady's fingers to a golden colour. Extract thin and thick milk from coconut. Boil cocums and extract 1 cup juice. Heat 2 tblsps. oil and fry onion, ginger, garlic and curry leaves till soft. Add thin coconut milk, cocum juice, chillies, lady's fingers, salt and turmeric powder. Cook for 5-7 minutes. Add thick milk and coriander leaves. Serve hot.

Vegetable Korma Curry

Ingredients (Serves 4)

- 100 grams each of french beans and potatoes, sliced
- 250 grams peas
- 100 grams tomatoes, grated
- 2 cloves, 2 cardamoms, 1 small cinnamon stick
- 1/2 sp. each of ginger and garlic paste
- 1 tblsp. poppy seeds
- 2 tblsps. each of grated coconut and curd
- 1 medium onion, grated
- 4 green chillies, slit
- Handful of chopped coriander leaves
- 1/4 tsp. turmeric powder
- Salt to taste

Preparation

Grind together poppy seeds and coconut. Heat 2 tblsps. oil and add the whole spices. Then add ginger, garlic, onions and the ground paste and fry till the oil comes out. Add the remaining ingredients. When the mixture turns dry, add 2 cups of water. Cook till the vegetables are done. Decorate with coriander leaves.

MOGHLAI MALAI KOFTA CURRY

Ingredients (Serves 4)

For Koftas

- 250 grams potatoes, boiled, peeled and mashed
- 100 grams grated cheese
- 2 tblsps. cornflour, 2 tblsps. curd
- 25 grams powdered cashewnuts
- 100 grams hard slab of butter, cut into small cubes.
- Salt to taste

Fur Curry

- 100 grams onions, grated
- 1/2 tsp. each of grated ginger and garlic
- 2 large tomatoes, grated
- 1/4 tsp. turmeric powder
- 1/2 tsp. each of garam masala and dhania-jeera powder
- 50 grams cream
- 2 rings of pineapple, cubed
- A few pieces of ripe mangoes
- Salt and chilli powder to taste

Preparation

Mix together potatoes, cheese, salt and cornflour. Form the mixture into small balls around a cube of butter. Deep fry the balls to a golden colour. Heat 4 tblsps. ghee and fry onion, ginger and garlic till soft. Add curd, spices tomatoes and salt and cook till thick. Then put in 2 cups of water and cook for 5 minutes. Pour the curry over the koftas. Pour cream over top and decorate with fruits.

Non-Vegetarian Curries
Murg Korma Curry

Ingredients (Serves 6)
- 1 medium chicken, disjointed
- 1/4 coconut,
- 100 grams onions, grated
- 1 cup curd
- 25 grams each of cashewnuts and charoli
- 2 tblsps. til seeds
- 1 tblsp. each of ginger and garlic paste
- 4 cloves, 4 cardamoms, 1 small cinnamon stick
- 2 bay leaves, 1/4 tsp. grated nutmeg
- 250 grams small potatoes, boiled and peeled
- 2 tblsp. lime juice
- Salt to taste

Preparation
Roast and grind together coconut, nuts and til. Mix the ground paste into the curd along with ginger, garlic and onions. Add to the mixture chicken and set aside it for 1 hour. Heat 100 grams oil and put in the whole spices. When they crackle, add the chicken along with the marinade. Cook over a slow fire till dry and the oil comes to the top. Then add the remaining spices and cover the contents with hot water. When the chicken is cooked, add lime juice and potatoes. Remove the curry from fire after a few minutes. Decorate with coriander leaves.

Nizami Curry

Ingredients (Serves 4)

- 1 medium chicken, disjointed
- 250 grams onions, grated
- 2 tblsps. each of ginger and garlic paste
- 25 grams fried cashewnuts
- 25 grams blanched, sliced and fried almonds
- Handful of coriander leaves
- A few mint leaves
- 2 cups of curd
- 1 tblsp. dhania-jeera powder
- 1 tsp. garam masala
- 1/4 tsp. turmeric powder
- 4 cloves, 4 cardamoms, 1 small cinnamon stick
- Salt and chilli powder to taste

Preparation

Powder cashewnuts. Heat 100 grams ghee. Add the whole spices, when they crackle, add ginger, onions and garlic. Fry to a golden colour. Add chicken, nuts, salt and chilli powder, turmeric and dhania-jeera powder, coriander and mint and curd. Cook the mixture over a slow fire till it becomes dry and oil floats to the top. Now cover the curry with hot water and cook till the chicken is done. Sprinkle garam masala on top of curry and serve.

SHEEKH KABAB CURRY

Ingredients (Serves 4)

For Curry

- 250 grams tomatoes, grated
- 100 grams onions, grated
- 1 tsp. of ginger and garlic paste
- 1 tsp. garam masala, 1/2 tsp. cardamom powder
- 1/2 cup cream, handful of coriander leaves
- 25 grams powdered cashewnuts
- 4 cloves, 4 cardamoms, 1 small cinnamon stick
- Salt and chilli powder to taste

For Kababs

- 500 grams minced mutton or kheema
- 1/2 cup firely sliced coriander leaves
- 4 green chillies, minced
- A few sliced mint leaves
- 1 tsp. grated ginger
- 4 tblsps. oil
- 1 tsp. cardamom seeds
- 1 tsp. garam masala
- 1 medium onion, grated
- 2 tblsps. grated raw papaya with skin
- Salt and chilli powder to taste

Preparation

Mix the kabab ingredients together. Shape the mixture into long sausages or cigarette shapes on well-greased skewers. Cook the sausages over charcoal or grill until well-browned on all the sides. Remove sausages from skewers. Heat 4 tblsps. oil, add whole spices. When they crackle add onions, ginger and garlic and fry till soft. Add tomatoes, cashewnuts, salt and remaining spices. Cook till the oil separates. Then add 2 cups of water. Cook for 5 minutes and pour the curry over the kababs. Also pour cream on top and decorate with chopped coriander leaves.

2

CURRIES OF KERALA

Kerala is one of the smallest states in South India. In this state, the backwaters and canals are fringed with tall coconut palms, so the people here use fresh coconut liberally in food. A unique feature of Kerala's food is that it is the only state in India which uses coconut oil for cooking. Rice is the staple food of Keralites and it is generally served with unusually delicious curries made of jackfruit, pineapple, bananas, various vegetables and fish and seafood which are available in plenty.

VEGETARIAN CURRIES

JACKFRUIT CURRY

Ingredients (Serves 6)

- 1 medium raw jackfruit
- 1 coconut, grated
- 1 medium onion and 1 small onion, finely sliced
- 6 green chillies
- 1/4 tsp. turmeric powder
- A few curry leaves
- 1 tsp. each of cumin and mustard seeds
- Salt to taste

Preparation

Set 1/4 grated coconut aside. Extract thin and thick milk from remaining coconut. Peel the jackfruit. Grease your hands and separate the fruit. Remove seeds and cut jackfruit into pieces. Grind grated coconut, medium onion, chillies and cumin seeds to a paste. Put the jackfruit in a pan along with turmeric, salt and thin coconut milk. When the vegetable is almost done, add the ground paste and curry leaves. Continue cooking till the vegetable is done. Now mix thick coconut milk into it. Heat to simmering and remove the curry form fire. Heat 1 tblsp. of oil and put in mustard seeds, when they stop tossing, add sliced onion and fry to a light golden colour. Put fried onions in the curry and serve hot.

MANGO CURRY

Ingredients (Serves 4)

- 3 raw mangoes, peeled and sliced
- A few pods of tamarind
- 1-1/2 cups of coconut milk
- 5 red chillies
- 1/4 tsp. turmeric powder
- 1 medium onion, finely sliced
- A few curry leaves
- 1 tsp. ground cumin seeds
- Salt to taste
- Jaggery if desired

Preparation

Grind tamarind and chillies to a paste. Heat 1 tblsp. oil and fry onions till soft. Add to the fried onions, ground paste and fry nicely. Add mangoes, all the spices and salt. Pour in the coconut milk and cook till the mangoes are done. Mix in the curry, grated jaggery and curry leaves and remove it from fire.

Mixed Vegetable Curry

Ingredients (Serves 5)

- 5 cups buttermilk
- 1/2 coconut, grated
- 1 tblsp. cumin seeds
- 1-inch piece of ginger
- 4 green chillies, slit
- 4 red chillies
- 3 tblsp. gramflour or besan
- 50 grams each of potato, pumpkin, french beans
- 1 drumstick, 1 raw banana
- A few curry leaves
- 1 tsp. each of mustard seeds and urad dal
- Salt to tast

Preparation

Peel and cut all the vegetables into 1-inch pieces. Grind coconut, cumin seeds, ginger and red chillies to a paste. Blend gramflour into buttermilk. Add salt and turmeric into vegetables with very little water and cook till almost done. Then put the ground paste in the vegetables and continue cooking till the vegetables are done. Pour in buttermilk. Boil till the curry is a little thick. Heat 2 tblsps. oil and put in mustard seeds, dal and curry leaves. When the dal turns red, pour this mixture into the curry.

PINEAPPLE CURRY

Ingredients (Serves 6)

- 1 ripe pineapple
- 4 red chillies, 3 red chillies, broken
- 1/4 tsp. each of mustard and fenugreek seeds
- A few curry leaves
- 1 glass of buttermilk
- 1/2 tsp. turmeric powder
- 1/2 coconut, grated
- 1 small onion, sliced
- 1 tsp. cumin seeds
- Salt to taste

Preparation

Peel the pineapple and remove all eyes carefully. Cut into slices. Remove the inside hard portion from pineapple slices and dice into pieces. Grind coconut, cumin seeds and green chillies to a paste. Place pineapple, salt and turmeric powder in a pan with very little water. Cover the pan tightly and cook till the pineapple is almost done. Then pour in buttermilk and add the ground paste. Continue cooking till the pineapple is tender. Mix in the curry leaves and remove from fire. Heat 2 tblsps. oil and add mustard and fenugreek seeds and red chillies. When the mixture turns brown, put it into the curry.

NON-VEGETARIAN CURRIES
MUTTON KORMA CURRY

Ingredients (Serves 4)
- 500 grams mutton, cut into serving portions
- 100 grams potatoes, boiled, peeled and cut into fours
- 1/2 coconut, ground
- 1 tblsp. each of ginger and garlic paste
- 1 tblsp. green chilli paste
- 2-inch piece of cinnamon, 4 cardamoms, 4 cloves
- 1/2 cup coriander leaves, chopped
- 1/4 tsp. turmeric powder
- 100 grams curd
- Salt to taste

Preparation
Powder together the spices. Mix them into curd along with ginger, garlic and chilli paste. Apply the paste on the mutton. Heat 50 grams oil and put mutton in it. Cook over a slow fire till the mutton turns dry. Fry to a red colour. Cover the mutton with hot water, then add coriander and coconut paste, and cook till mutton is tender. Finally put in potatoes and cook for a few more minutes. Serve hot.

COCONUT MEAT CURRY

Ingredients (Serves 4)

- 500 grams mutton, cut into serving portions
- 2 potatoes, boiled, peeled and cut into fours
- 2 medium onions, grated
- 1 tblsp. grated ginger
- 1 cup thick, 2 cups thin coconut milk
- 1/2 tsp. each of mustard and cumin seeds
- 4 cloves, 4 cardamoms
- 1 small stick of cinnamon
- 8 peppercorns, 4 green chillies, minced
- A few curry leaves
- 2 tblsps. vinegar
- Salt to taste

Preparation

Put mutton, onions, thin milk, ginger, green chillies, curry, leaves, spices, salt and vinegar in a vessel and cook till the mutton is tender. Add potatoes and thick milk and heat the mixture to simmering. Remove the curry from fire. Heat 2 tblsps. oil and fry mustard and cumin seeds. Pour the hot oil over the curry and serve hot.

CHICKEN CURRY

Ingredients (Serves 5)
- 1 medium chicken, disjointed
- 2 large onions, grated
- 5 green chillies, minced
- 1 tblsp. grated ginger
- 1 cup thick, 2 cups thin coconut milk
- 2 tblsp. vinegar
- A few curry leaves
- 1 tblsp. coriander seeds
- 4 red chillies, 1 tblsp. peppercorns
- 1/2 tsp. each of mustard, cumin and fenugreek seeds
- 2 tsp. poppy seeds
- 1/2 tsp. turmeric powder
- 1 large onion
- 8 flakes of garlic
- 2-inch piece of cinnamon
- 3 cloves, 3 cardamoms
- 1 tsp. anise seeds
- Salt to taste

Preparation

Roast and powder together whole onion, garlic, red chillies and all the whole spices. Heat 100 grams oil and fry grated ginger, chillies and onions till soft. Add ground paste to the mixture and fry till the oil comes out. Put in chicken and cook till dry. Fry to a golden colour. Add thin coconut milk and cook till the chicken is cooked. Add thick milk, curry leaves and lime juice. Heat the curry to simmering and remove if from fire.

COCONUT FISH CURRY

Ingredients (Serves 4)

- 500 grams any white-fleshed fish, cleaned and sliced
- 2 medium onions, grated
- 1 tsp. each of ginger and garlic paste
- 4 green chillies, slit
- 1 tblsp. vinegar
- A few curry leaves
- 1/2 cup thick and 2 cups thin coconut milk
- 1/2 tsp. turmeric powder
- Salt and chilli powder to taste

Preparation

Fry the fish slices lightly. Heat 2 tblsps. oil and fry ginger, garlic and onions till soft. Add to this mixture fish and 1/2 cup of thin coconut milk, salt, vinegar and turmeric powder. Cook the contents over a slow fire till the gravy is almost dry. Pour in remaining thin coconut milk and cook till the gravy is almost thick. Finally add thick coconut milk and curry leaves. Heat to simmering and remove the curry from fire.

PRAWN AND TAMARIND CURRY

Ingredients (Serves 4)

- 500 grams prawns, cleaned, shelled and deveined
- 1 lime-sized ball of tamarind
- 1/2 coconut, 2 medium onions
- 1 tblsp. coriander seeds, 1/2 tsp. fenugreek seeds
- 8 red chillies
- A few curry leaves
- Salt to taste

Preparation

Cover tamarind with 2 cups of hot water and then squeeze out the pulp. Fry rest of the ingredients except prawns in a little oil and grind the mixture to a paste. Heat tamarind, add prawns and ground paste and cook till the prawns are done.

3

CURRIES OF TAMILNADU

Tamilnadu is populated largely with vegetarians. Therefore they prepare many delicious curries of vegetables and dals. The curries here are usually hotter than the ones prepared in the North. Generally, Tamilians use either coconut milk or coconut paste as base for their curries. Tamil curries are delightfully delicious, and with rice they make a most satisfying meal.

VEGETARIAN CURRIES
LADY'S FINGER CURRY

Ingredients (Serves 2)

- 250 grams lady's finger, sliced
- 1 big onion, grated
- 1 tsp. each of garlic and ginger paste
- 2 tblsps. grated coconut
- 4 green chillies
- Handful of coriander leaves
- 20 grams tamarind soaked in 1 cup water for 5 minutes
- 1 tblsp. dhania-jeera powder
- 1/4 tsp. turmeric powder
- 1/2 tsp. mustard seeds
- A few curry leaves
- Salt and chilli powder to taste

Preparation

Grind together onion, ginger, garlic, coconut, chillies and coriander leaves. Fry the lady's fingers to a light golden colour. Heat 2 tblsps. oil and fry the ground paste till the oil comes out. Add spices, salt and the lady's fingers. Squeeze out the tamarind water and pour into the lady's fingers along with 1/2 cup water. Cook the mixture for 5-7 minutes. Heat 1 tsp. oil and fry mustard seeds and curry leaves. Pour this oil mixture over the curry and serve hot.

BEETROOT CURRY

Ingredients (Serves 4)

- 150 grams arhar or tuvar dal
- 2 big beetroots, boiled, peeled and cubed
- 1 medium onions, grated
- 1 medium tomato, sliced
- 1 lime-sized ball of tamarind
- A few curry leaves
- 1/2 tsp. ginger and garlic paste
- 4 green chillies, slit
- 1/4 tsp. turmeric powder
- 1/2 tsp. garam masala
- Salt and chilli powder to taste

Preparation

Soak tamarind in hot water for 5 minutes, then squeeze out the tamarind water. Boil dal along with salt and turmeric powder till soft. Mash the boiled dal to a paste. Heat 2 tblsps. oil, add a pinch of asafoetida, curry leaves, ginger, garlic and onions. Fry the mixture till oil comes out. Add dal, chillies, tamarind, tomato pieces and beetroots. Cook for 10 minutes over a slow fire. Sprinkle garam masala on top.

COCONUT AND TOMATO CURRY

Ingredients (Serves 4)

- 250 grams tomatoes, grated
- 150 grams arhar or tuvar dal
- 100 grams grated coconut
- 1/2 tsp. mustard seeds
- 4 green chillies, slit
- A few curry leaves
- 1/4 tsp. turmeric powder
- 1/2 inch piece of ginger, grated
- Handful of chopped coriander leaves
- A big pinch of asafoetida
- Salt and chilli powder to taste

Preparation

Grind coconut and ginger to a paste. Boil dal in water with turmeric powder and salt till the dal becomes very soft. Mash the boiled dal to a paste. Heat 4 tblsps. oil and add mustard seeds and asafoetida. When the seeds stop tossing, add coconut paste, curry leaves. Fry nicely and add tomatoes. When the mixture turns thick, add dal and chillies and 2 cups of water. Cook till the curry turns a little thick. Decorate with coriander leaves.

BRINJAL CURRY

Ingredients (Serves 2)

- 250 grams brinjal, sliced
- 4 red chillies
- 1 tsp. each of coriander seeds, sesame seeds and chana dal
- A pinch of asafoetida
- 10 grams tamarind
- 1/4 tsp. turmeric powder
- 1/4 coconut, grated
- A few curry leaves
- 1/2 tsp. mustard seeds
- Salt to taste

Preparation

Fry chillies, coriander and sesame seeds, coconut and til in little oil to a red colour, then grind this mixture to a coarse paste. Cover tamarind in hot water for 5 minutes and then squeeze out the pulp. Heat 3 tblsps. oil and add mustard seeds. When the seeds stop popping, put in the brinjal slices, curry leaves and salt. Fry until the brinjal slices start changing colour. Add the remaining ingredients. Cook till dry. Pour in 2 cups of water, cook again for 5 more minutes. Decorate with coriander leaves.

PAPAYA CURRY

Ingredients (Serves 6)
- 1 medium raw papaya, peeled and sliced
- 1 medium onion, finely sliced
- 4 green chillies, slit
- 4 flakes of garlic, a 1-inch piece of ginger
- 1 tsp. cumin seeds
- 4 red chillies ,10 peppercorns
- A few curry leaves
- 1/2 coconut
- 1/4 tsp. turmeric powder
- 1 big tomato, grated
- Salt to taste

Preparation
Grind coconut, peppercorns, red chillies, garlic, ginger and cumin seeds to a paste. Heat 2 tblsps. oil and fry the onions lightly. Put in the fried onions, the ground paste, tomatoes and spices, and cook. When oil comes out, add papaya and 1 glass of water. Cook till the papaya is done. Mix in the curry leaves and serve hot.

Methi Bhaji Curry

Ingredients (Serves 4)

- 1 big bunch fenugreek leaves, cleaned and sliced
- 3 cups of buttermilk
- 1/2 tsp. mustard seeds
- 1/4 tsp. fenugreek seeds
- 4 tsp. gramflour
- 1/4 tsp. turmeric powder
- 1 big onion, minced
- 3 green chillies, minced
- 1 tsp. grated ginger
- Salt and chilli powder to taste

Preparation

Heat 2 tblsps. oil, add fenugreek and mustard seeds. When the seeds stop tossing, add ginger, onion and chillies and fry till soft. Then add to methi, salt, turmeric and chilli powder. Cook till the leaves are done. Mix gramflour in buttermilk and pour in the methi mixture, cook till the gravy is little thick.

METHI AND DAL CURRY

Ingredients (Serves 6)

- 1 cup cooked tuvar dal
- 1 big bunch of fenugreek leaves, cleaned and sliced
- 1 cup finely grated coconut
- 1/2 tsp. mustard seeds
- 1/4 tsp. turmeric powder
- 4 red chillies, broken
- Salt to taste

Preparation

Heat 2 tblsps. oil and put in mustard seeds and chillies. When the mustard seeds stop popping, add methi, salt and turmeric. When the leaves are cooked, add coconut, dal and 2 cups of water. Cook for 5 minutes. Serve hot.

DAL CURRY

Ingredients (Serves 6)

For Dal Diamond

- 250 grams tuvar or arhar dal
- 1 tsp. each of grated ginger and garlic
- 6 green chillies
- Handful of coriander leaves
- 2 medium onions, minced
- Salt and chilli powder to taste

For Curry

- 1 lime-sized ball of tamarind
- 4 red chillies.
- 1 tblsp. coriander seeds
- A few curry leaves
- 2 medium onions
- 2 big tomatoes, grated
- 4 flakes of garlic
- 1/4 tsp. each of mustard and cumin seeds
- 1/4 coconut
- Handful of coriander leaves
- Salt to taste

Preparation

Soak dal in water for a couple of hours. Drain water and grind dal to a coarse paste with ginger chillies, garlic and onions. Mix salt, lime juice and coriander leaves in the dal paste. Make a 1/2 an inch thick layer of the paste in a greased thali. Steam it till it turns firm. Remove from fire, cut into diamond pieces. Deep fry the diamond pieces to a golden colour. Grind coconut, chillies, coriander seeds and garlic to a paste. Heat 2 tblsps. oil and fry the ground paste till oil comes out. Add tomatoes, salt and turmeric powder. Cook till the tomatoes turn soft. In the meanwhile, soak tamarind in hot water for 5 minutes and squeeze out the pulp. Pour tamarind water along with 2 cups of water into the tomatoes. Heat the mixture to boiling, then reduce heat and add the dal pieces. Cook for 5 minutes Heat 2 tblsps. oil and put in mustard and cumin seeds, curry leaves and 2 broken red chillies. When the seeds stop popping, pour the oil mixture over the curry. Decorate with coriander leaves.

DAL KOFTA CURRY

Ingredients (Serves 4)

For Koftas

- 1 cup tuvar or arhar dal
- 1/2 tsp. each of grated ginger and garlic
- 1 small onion
- Handful of coriander leaves
- Salt to taste

For Curry

- 4 cups of buttermilk
- 4 green chillies, slit
- 1/4 coconut, grated
- 1 tsp. grated ginger
- 1 tsp. each of coriander and cumin seeds and chana dal
- 1/4 tsp. fenugreek seeds
- A few curry leaves
- Handful of coriander leaves
- 1/2 tsp. each of mustard seeds and turmeric powder
- Salt to taste

Preparation

Wash and soak dal for a few hours. Drain the water and grind dal to a coarse paste along with ginger, garlic, chillies and onions. Mix salt and coriander leaves in the paste. Form the paste into small balls and steam the balls for 20 minutes. Grind chana dal, coconut, coriander, cumin and fenugreek seeds to a paste. Mix the paste into the buttermilk along with turmeric and salt. Place buttermilk on fire and put in the green chillies and dal koftas. Boil for 2-3 and remove the curry form fire. Heat 2 tblsps. oil and put in mustard seeds and curry leaves. When the seeds stop bursting, pour the oil over curry. Serve decorated with coriander leaves.

VADAIS COCONUT CURRY

Ingredients (Serves 4)

For Vadais

- 2 cups chana dal
- 1/2 cup sliced fenugreek leaves
- 4 small onions, minced
- 4 green chilies, minced
- 4 flakes of garlic, minced
- Salt to taste

For Curry

- 2 cups thick and 3 cups thin coconut milk
- 6 flakes of garlic
- 1 tblsp. poppy seeds
- A few curry leaves
- Handful of chopped coriander leaves
- 2 cardamoms, 8 peppercorns, 2 cloves
- 2 green chillies, minced
- 4 small onions, minced
- 1 tblsp. fried raisins, 12 cashewnuts, fried
- Salt to taste

Preparation

Wash and soak dal in water for a few hours. Drain the water and grind dal to a coarse paste. Mix in all the vadai ingredients. Form the mixture into small round vadas with a hole at the centre on a wet cloth. Deep fry vadas to a golden colour. Grind garlic, poppy seeds and whole spices to a paste. Heat 4 tblsps. oil and fry onions, chillies and curry leaves to a golden colour. Put in the ground paste and fry nicely. Pour on thin coconut milk and bring the mixture slowly to a boil. Reduce heat to simmering and add vadas and remaining spices. Simmer for 2 minutes, pour in thick milk. After 2 minutes, remove the curry form fire and add cashewnuts, raisins and chopped coriander leaves.

VADAI CURD CURRY

Ingredients (Serves 6)

For Vadais

- 250 grams tuvar or arhar dal
- 1 coconut, finely grated
- 6 green chillies
- 1 small bunch of coriander leaves
- 1 tsp. grated ginger
- 1 small onion
- Salt to taste

For Curry

- 250 grams sour curd
- 4 green chillies, slit
- 1 small bunch of coriander leaves
- 1/2 tsp. each of cumin and mustard seeds
- 1-inch piece of ginger
- 1/2 tsp. turmeric powder
- 1 tblsp. urad dal
- 2 tblsp. grated coconut
- Salt to taste

Preparation

Wash and soak dal for a few hours in water. Drain water and grind dal to a coarse paste. Mince together rest of the vadai ingredients and mix with the dal along with salt. Form the minced mixture into round vadais and steam them till firm. Soak urad dal for a few minutes. Drain water and grind dal to a paste along with rest of the curry ingredients. Beat curd with 2 cups of water. Heat 3 tblsps. oil and fry the ground paste till oil comes out. Put the fried paste in curd along with curry leaves, green chillies and salt. Then put in the vadais and simmer for 5-7 minutes. Decorate with coriander leaves.

4
MANGLOREAN CURRIES

Manglore is near Mysore in Karnataka. This region abounds in coconut trees, therefore coconut is used in almost all Manglorean recipes. Manglorean Christians are non-vegetarians and they prepare well-seasoned and highly spiced meat, chicken, pork, fish, prawn and egg curries which are appetizingly served and enjoyed by a wide section of people.

Non-Vegetarian Curries

Mangalore
Egg Curry

Ingredients (Serves 4)

- 4 hard-boiled eggs, shelled and cut into halves, lengthwise
- 2 medium potatoes, boiled, peeled, cubed and fried lightly
- 4 red and 2 green chillies
- 1/2 tsp. cumin seeds
- 1/4 tsp. turmeric powder
- 1 medium onion
- 1 tsp. each of grated ginger and garlic
- 1 tblsp. vinegar
- 1 tsp. sugar
- 2 big tomatoes, grated
- Handful of sliced coriander leaves
- Salt to taste

Preparation

Grind together ginger, garlic and all the spices to a paste in vinegar. Heat 2 tblsps. oil and fry the ground paste nicely. Put in sugar, salt and tomatoes. Cook the mixture till the tomatoes turn soft. Then put in 2 cups of water, bring the curry to a boil. Reduce heat and put eggs in the curry. Simmer till the gravy turns a little thick. Decorate with coriander leaves.

Prawn and Brinjal Curry

Ingredients (Serves 6)

- 500 grams prawns, shelled and deveined
- 1 large brinjal, sliced
- 1 tblsp. each of coriander and cumin seeds
- 1/2 tsp. turmeric powder
- 2 tblsp. finely sliced coconut
- 2 big tomatoes, grated
- 2 cups thin and 1 cup thick coconut milk
- 1 big onion, minced
- 1 tsp. each of ginger and garlic paste
- Salt and lemon juice to taste
- Handful of chopped coriander leaves
- Salt to taste

Preparation

Fry sliced onion to a red colour. Powder all the spices. Apply salt and turmeric on prawns and set aside for half an hour. Heat 4 tblsps. oil and put in it onions, garlic and ginger, fry till soft. Add tomatoes and all the spices and cook till dry. Then add prawns, brinjals and thin coconut milk. Cook over a slow fire till the vegetable and prawns are done. Mix in thick coconut milk and remove the curry from fire. Decorate with fried coconut, coriander leaves and sprinkle lime juice on top.

MUTTON CURRY

Ingredients (Serves 5)

- 500 grams mutton, cut into serving portions
- 1 lime-sized ball of tamarind
- 12 small potatoes, 12 small onions
- 2 carrots, 1 large tomato grated
- 250 grams green peas, shelled
- 1/2 tsp. turmeric powder, 1/4 coconut
- 6 red chillies
- 1 tsp. each of ginger and garlic paste
- 1 tblsp. each of cumin and coriander seeds
- 1 big onion, minced
- 1/4 tsp. mustard seeds
- Salt to taste

Preparation

Grind onion, garlic, chillies and all the spices to a paste. Apply the paste on mutton and set it aside for 1 hour. Cover tamarind with hot water for 5 minutes and then squeeze out the pulp. Heat 100 grams oil and fry in it the mutton to a red colour. Cover the fried mutton with hot water. Add salt and tomato and cook till the mutton is half done. Put in the vegetables and tamarind and continue cooking till the mutton and vegetables both are done. Serve hot.

LIVER AND POTATO CURRY

Ingredients (Serves 4)

- 500 grams liver, washed and cubed
- 1 lime-sized ball of tamarind
- 2 medium potatoes, boiled, peeled, cubed and fried lightly.
- 2 medium onions
- 4 cloves, 1 small cinnamon stick
- 1/4 coconut
- 6 flakes of garlic
- 1 tsp. cumin seeds
- 1 tblsp. coriander seeds
- 1/2 tsp. mustard seeds
- 1 tsp. anise seeds or saunf
- Salt and chilli powder to taste

Preparation

Cover tamarind with hot water for 5 minutes and then squeeze out its pulp. Grind onion, coconut, garlic and all the spices to a paste. Boil liver in salt water till it becomes tender and dry. Heat 3 tblsps. oil and fry in it the ground paste till oil floats out. Add liver, potatoes and tamarind. Cook for 5 minutes, decorate with coriander leaves.

HOT AND SPICY PORK CURRY

Ingredients (Serves 8)

- 1 kilo pork, cut into serving portions
- 10 red chillies, 1 medium onion
- 1 tsp. turmeric powder
- 1 lime-sized ball of tamarind
- 6 flakes of garlic, 8 peppercorns, 5 cloves
- 1 small cinnamon stick
- 2 tblsps. vinegar, 1 tblsp. sugar, 3 tblsps. brandy
- 150 grams small potatoes, boiled and peeled
- Salt to taste

Preparation

Grind chillies, onion, tamarind, garlic and all the whole spices to make a paste. Heat 100 grams oil and fry in it the ground paste till the oil comes out. Add pork and fry to a golden colour. Then add remaining ingredients except potatoes. Mix well and cover the mixture with boiling water. When the pork is done, put in the potatoes. Cook for a few minutes and remove the curry from fire. Serve hot.

IMPORTANT INGREDIENTS USED IN CURRY PREPARATION AND THEIR MEDICINAL VALUE

Garlic

Garlic is a powerful antiseptic, and therefore it kills bacteria. It improves the voice and eyesight. It is a tonic to the hair and is useful in cough, gastric troubles, worms, heart disease, asthma, acidity, piles, chronic fever, loss of appetite, constipation, diabetes and tuberculosis. It also has properties of reducing high blood pressure.

Ginger

Ginger is good for eyes and throat. A small piece of ginger taken with a pinch of black salt before meals eliminates gas. It gives freedom from cough and cold and is also helpful in cardiac disorders, odema, urinary trouble, jaundice, piles and asthma. Ginger juice is also said to prevent the malignancy of the tongue and the throat. Toothache is also relieved if a piece of ginger is rubbed on the painful tooth.

Onions

From the medicinal point of view, white onions are more beneficial to the body than other varieties. They increase virility and induce sleep. They are good for curing tuberculosis, piles, leprosy, swelling and blood impurities. One is saved from sunstroke if one regularly eats raw onions during hot season. Eating raw onion in the morning and at bedtime is good for jaundice patients.

Coriander leaves

Coriander leaves are mostly used for decorating a dish or preparing chutney. They give a special flavour to food. Coriander is not only fragrant and appetizing but also a good digestive aid. It has a cooling effect on our body, and is good for vision and agreeable to the heart.

Mint

Mint is usually made into chutneys or sometimes put in non-vegetarian dishes. It is not only palatable and appetizing but is also good for heart. It expels gas and is useful in cough, dysentery, gastroenteritis and diarrhoea.

Vegetables

They are extremely rich source of minerals, enzymes and vitamins. Their nutritional value varies according to their different parts. Leaves, stems and fruits are rich sources of minerals, vitamins, water and roughage, whereas seeds are high in carbohydrates and proteins. Greener and fresher the vegetables, higher their vitamin content. Therefore always go in for fresh vegetables available in the market.

Eggs

Eggs are a valuable source of animal proteins and next to milk in providing nutrition. Egg yolk contains Iron, B vitamins, calcium and a considerable amount of proteins. White portion contains vitamin B and more than half the amount of proteins in egg. Patients of high cholesterol and heart disease should not eat yolks but go only for whites of the egg.

Fish

Fish rates high in nutritional value. It supplies proteins which are more easily digestible than the proteins of meat. Fish gives fat, vitamins A & D and minerals like iodine and copper to the body. Fish is a low-fat form of proteins. Sardines, mackerel and other oily fish contain omega-3 fatty acids that help clear the body of cholesterol.

Meat & Poultry

These are very rich sources of proteins. Besides proteins they are rich in fats, vitamin A and phosphorus. However, kidney and liver are low in fat. Just one helping a day of meat or fish is enough for the daily body requirement of proteins.

FOODGRAINS Cookery Glossary

English	Spiked millet	Barley	Jowar	Italian millet	Maize (dry)	Oatmeal	Ragi
Hindi	Bajra	Jau	Juar-janera	Kangri	Makai	Jai	Okra
Tamil	Cambu	Barli arisi	Cholam	Thenai	Muka cholam	–	Ragi
Telugu	Gantelu	Barli biyyam	Jonnalu	Korralu	Mekka jonnalu	–	Chollu
Marathi	Bajri	Juv	Jwari	Rala	Muka	–	Nachni
Bengali	Bajra	Job	Juar	Syamadhan kangni	Sukna paka bhutta	Jai	–
Gujarati	Bajri	Jau	Juar	Ral kang	Makai	–	Ragi bhav
Malayalam	Kamboo	Yavam	Cholam	Thina	Unakku cholam	Oat mavu	Moothari (korra)
Kannada	–	–	Jola	–	Vonugida musikinu	Jolu	Ragi
Kashmiri	Baajr'u	Wushku	–	Shol	Makka'y	–	–

Contd...

English	Rice (raw)	Rice (parboiled)	Rice (white)	Rice (black)	Rice flakes	Rice (puffed)	Samai
Hindi	Arwa chawal	Usna chawal	Safed chaval	Chaval (kala)	Chowla	Murmura	Kutki, Sanwali
Tamil	Pachai arisi	Puzhungal arisi	Vellai puttu arisi	Karuppu puttu arisi	Arisi aval	Arisia pori	Samai
Telugu	Pachi biyyam	Uppudu biyyam	Thella biyyam	Nalla biyyam	Atukulu	Murmuralu	–
Marathi	Tandool	Tandool ukda	–	–	Pohe	Murmure	Sava
Bengali	Atap chowl	Siddha chowl	–	–	Chaler khood	Muri	Kangni
Gujarati	Hatna	Ukadelloo chokha	–	–	Pohva	Mumra	–
Malayalam	Pacchari	Puzhungal ari	Velutha puttari	Krutha puttari	Avil	Pori	–
Kannada	Kotnuda	Kotnuda	–	–	Avalukki	–	Puri
Kashmiri	–	–	–	–	–	–	–

Contd...

English	Semolina	Vermicelli	Wheat (whole)	Wheat flour (whole)	Wheat flour (refined)	Wheat (broken)
Hindi	Sooji	Siwain	Gehun	Atta	Maida	Daliya
Tamil	Ravai	Semiya	Godumai	Muzhu godmai ma	Maida mavu	Godhumbi ravai
Telugu	Rawa	Semiya	Godhumalu	Godhum pindi	Maidha pindi	Dinchina gadhumalu
Marathi	–	Shevaya	Gahu	Gahu kuneek	Gahu kuneek	Gavache satva
Bengali	Suji	Sewai	Gomasta	Atta	Maida	Bhanga gom
Gujarati	–	–	Ghau	Ato	–	Fadia ghaun
Malayalam	Rava	Semiya	Muzhu gothambu	Gothambu mavu	Maidu tha gothambu mavu	Gothumbu ari
Kannada	–	Shavige	Godhi	Godhi	Hittu madia	Kuttida Godhi
Kashmiri	–	Ku' nu'	–	–	–	–

VEGETABLES

English	Ash gourd	Bitter gourd	Bottle gourd	Brinjal	Broad beans	Cabbage	Capsicum
Hindi	Safed petha	Karela	Chia	Baingan	Sem	Bandhgobi	Simla mirch
Bengali	Chal kumdo	karala	Laoo	Begoon	Sheem	Badha kopee	Lonka
Assamese	Lao bishesh	–	Jati lao	Bengena	Urahi	Bondhakobi	Kashmiri jalakai
Oriya	Pani kakkaru	–	Lau	Baigana	Shimba	Patrokobi	Simla lonka
Marathi	Kohala	Karle	Dudhi	Wangi	Ghewda	Pan kobi	Bhopli mirchi
Gujarati	Petha	Karela	Dudhi	Ringna	Papdi	Kobi	Simla marchan
Telugu	Boodie gumadi	Kakara	Sorakaya	Vankaya	Pedda chikkudu	Kosu	Pedda mirappa
Kannada	Budu gumbala	Hagalkai	Sorekai	Badanekai	Chapparadavare	Kosu	Donne minasinakai
Tamil	Pooshanikkai	Pavakkai	Suraikai	Kaththarikai	Avaraikai	Muttaikosu	Kuda milakai
Malayalam	Kumbalanga	Kaypakka	Cheraikai	Vazhutheninga	Amarakai	Muttakose	Parangi mulagu
Kashmiri	Masha'fy al	Karelu	–	Waangun	–	Bandgobhi	–

Contd...

48

English	Carrot	Cauliflower	Cluster beans	Colocasia	Coriander leaves	Cucumber	Curry leaves
Hindi	Gajar	Phulgobi	Guar ki phalli	Arvi	Hara Dhania	Khira	Kadi patta
Bengali	Gujar	Foolcopy	Jhar sim	–	Dhonay pata	Sasha	Curry pata
Assamese	Gajor	Phoolkobi	–	Kochu	Dhania paat	–	Narasingha paat
Oriya	Gajar	Phulakobi	–	–	Dhania patra	–	Bhrusanga patta
Marathi	Gajar	Fulkobi	Govari	Alu kanda	Kothimbir	Kakari	Kadhi patta
Gujarati	Gajar	Fool kobi	Govar	Alvi	Kothmir	Kakdi	Mitho limdo
Telugu	Gajjara	Cauliflower	Goruchikkudu kayalu	Chamadumpa	Kothimeera	Dosakaya	Karivepaku
Kannada	Gajjari	Hookosu	Gorikayi	Keshave	Kottambari soppu	Southaikayi	Karibevu
Tamil	Carrot	Koveppu	Kothavarangai	Seppann kizhangu	Koththamali ilaigal	Kakkarikkai	Karveppilai
Malayalam	Carrot	Coliflower	Kothavara	Chembu	Kothamalli ila	Vellari	Kariveppila
Kashmiri	–	Phoolgobhi	–	–	–	Laa'r	–

Contd...

English	Drumstick	French beans	Garlic	Ginger (fresh)	Green chillies	Jackfruit	Lady's finger
Hindi	Sahjan ki phali	Pharsbeen	Lassan	Adrak	Hari mirch	Kathal	Bhindi
Bengali	Sajane dauta	French beans	Rasoon	Ada (tatka)	Kancha lonka	Echore	Dhanroce
Assamese	Sajina	Faras been	Naharoo	Ada (kesa)	Kesa jalakia	–	Bhendi
Oriya	Sajana chhuin	French beans	Rasuna	Ada (kancha)	Kancha lonka	–	Bhendi
Marathi	Shevgyachya shenga	Farasbi	Lasun	Aale	Hirya mirchya	Kawla phanas	Bhendi
Gujarati	Saragvani shing	Fansi	Lasan	Adu	Lila marcha	Phunas	Bhinda
Telugu	Munagakayalu	French chikkudu	Vellulli	Allam (pachchi)	Pachchi mirapakayalu	Letha panasa	Bendakaaya
Kannada	Nuggekai	Avare	Bellulli	Ashi Shunti	Hasi menasinakai	Yele halasu	Bendekai
Tamil	Murungaikai	Beans	Ulli Poondu	Inji	Pachchai milagai	Pila pinchu	Vendaikai
Malayalam	Muringakkaya	Beans	Veluthulli	Inji	Pachamulagu	Idichakka	Vendakka
Kashmiri	–	–	Ruhan	–	Myool martsu waungun	–	Bindu

English	Lettuce	Lemon	Mint leaves	Onion	Parwal	Peas	Plantain flower	Plantain green
Hindi	Salad ke patte	Nimbu	Pudina	Pyaz	Parwal	Matar	Kele ka phool	Kacha kela
Bengali	Lettuce	Lebu	Poodina pata	Pyaz	Potol	Motor	Mocha	Kancha kala
Assamese	Laipaat	Nemu	Podina	–	Patol	Motormah	–	–
Oriya	Lettuce	Lembu	Podana patra	–	Potala	Matar	–	–
Marathi	Saladchi paane	Limbu	Pudina	Kanda	–	Matar	Kel phool	Kele
Gujarati	Lettuce	Limbu	Fudino	Dungli	–	Vatana	Kelphool	Kela
Telugu	Lettuce koora	Nimma	Pudhina koora	Nirulli	–	Bathanedu	Aratipuwu	Arati kayi
Kannada	Lettuce soppu	Nimbu	Pudina sopu	Erulli	–	Betani	Balo mothu	Bala kayi
Tamil	Lettuce keerai	Elumicham pazham	Pudhinaa	Vengayam	–	Pattani	Vazhaippu	Vazhaikkai
Malayalam	Uvarcheera	Cherunaranga	Pudhinaa	Ulli	–	Pattani Payaru	Vazhappoo	Vazhakka
Kashmiri	Salaad	–	–	Gandu	–	Matar	–	–

Contd...

English	Plantain stem	Potato	Radish	Red pumpkin	Ridge gourd	Snake gourd	Sweet potato	Yam elephant
Hindi	Kele ka tana	Aloo	Muli	Sitaphal	Torai	–	Shakarkand	Zaminkand
Bengali	Thor	Aloo	Mulo	Ronga Koomra	Jhinge	Chichinga	Rangalu	Kham aloo
Assamese	–	Alu	–	Ronga lao	–	–	–	Kaath aloo
Oriya	–	Alu	–	Kakharu	–	–	–	Deshi alu
Marathi	Kelecha khunt	Batate	Mula	Lal bhopla	Dodka	Pudwal	Ratale	Suran
Gujarati	Kelanu thed	Batata	Mula	Kolu	Turai	Pandola	Sakkaria	Suran
Telugu	Arati davva	Bangaala dumpa	Mullangi	Erra gummadi	Beerakai	Potlakayi	Dumpalu	Kanda dumpa
Kannada	Dindu	Aalugadde	Mullangi	Kempu kumbala	Heeraikai	Padavalai	Genasu	Suvarnagadde
Tamil	Vazhaithandu	Urulaikizhangu	Mullangi	Parangikai	Pirkkankai	Podalangai	Sarkarai valli kizhangu	Chenai kizhangu
Malayalam	Vazhappindi	Uralakkizhangu	Mullangi	Chuvappu mathan	Pecchinga	Padavalanga	Chakkara kizhangu	Chena
Kashmiri	–	Oloo	Muj	Paarimal	Turrelu	–	–	–

PULSES

English	Bengal gram (whole)	Bengal gram (split)	Black gram (split)	Black gram (whole)	Cornflour	Cow gram`	Green gram (whole)
Hindi	Chana	Chana dal	Urad dal	Sabat urad	Makai ka atta	Lobia (bada)	Moong
Bengali	Chola	Banglar chhola	Mashkolair dal	Mashkolai dal	Bhoottar maida	Barbati	Mug
Assamese	–	Buttor dail	Matir dail (phola)	Matir dail (gota)	Moida	–	–
Oriya	–	Buta (chhota)	Biri (phala)	Biri (gota)	Makka atta	–	–
Marathi	Hurbhura	Chana dal	Udid dal	Udid	Makyache pith	Kuleeth	Mug
Gujarati	Chana	Chana nidaal	Adad ni dal	Adad	Makai no lot	–	Mag
Telugu	Sanagalu	Senaga pappu	Mina pappu	Minu mulu	Mokkajonnalu (pindi)	Ada chandalu	Pesalu
Kannada	Kadale	Kadale bela	Uddina bela	Uddu	Musukinajolada hittu	Thadaguni	Hesaru kalu
Tamil	Muzhu kadalai	Kadalai paruppu	Ulutham paruppu	Ulundhu	Chola Maavu	Karamani	Pachai payaru
Malayalam	Kadala	Kadala parippu	Uzhunnu parrippu	Uzhunnu	Cholapodi	Payar	Cherupayaru
Kashmiri	Chanu	–	Maha	–	–	–	Muang

Contd...

English	Green gram (split)	Horse gram	Kesari dal	Kidney beans	Red gram	Red lentils	Soya bean
Hindi	Moong dal	Kulthi	Lang dal	Rajma	Arhar dal	Masoor dal	Bhat
Bengali	–	Kulthi kalai	Khesari	Barbati beej	Arhar dal	Lal masoor (bhanga)	Gari kalai
Assamese	–	–	–	Markhowa urahi	Rahor dail	Masoor dail (phola)	–
Oriya	–	–	–	Baragudi chhuin	Harada dali	Masura dali (phala)	–
Marathi	–	Kuleeth	Lakh dal	–	Tur dal	Masur dal	Soya
Gujarati	–	Kuleeth	Lakh	–	Tuver dal	Masur dal	Soya
Telugu	Pesaru pappu	Ulavalu	Lanka pappu	–	Kandi pappu	Missu pappu	–
Kannada	Hesare bele	Huruli	–	–	Togar bele	Masur bele	–
Tamil	Pasi paruppu	Kollu	Vattuparuppu	–	Thuvaram parappu	Massor paruppu	–
Malayalam	Cherupayar parippu	Muthira	–	–	Thuvara parippu	Masoor parippu	Soya bean
Kashmiri	–	–	–	–	–	Musur	–

FRUITS AND DRY FRUITS

English	Almond	Coconut	Currants	Dates	Dry plums
Hindi	Badam	Nariyal	Mungaqqa	Khajur	Alu bukhara
Bengali	Badam	Narcole	Manaca	Khejoor	Sookno kool
Assamese	Badam	Narikol	Kismis	Khejur	Sukan bogori
Oriya	Badaam	Nadia	Kala kismis	Khajura	Barakoli jateeya phala
Marathi	Badam	Naral	Manuka	Khajur	Alubhukar
Gujarati	Badam	Naliyer	Kalli draksh	Khajoor	Suka Plum
Telugu	Badam	Kobbari kaaya	Endu nalla dhraksha	Kharjoora pandu	–
Kannada	Badami	Tenginakai	Dweepa dharakshi-kappu	Kharjoora	–
Tamil	Badam/vadhumai	Thengai	Karumdhraakshai	Perichampazham	Aalpacota ular pazham
Malayalam	Badam	Nalikeram/Thenga	Karuthamurthiri	Eethapazham	–

Contd...

English	Guavas	Lemon	Orange	Raisins	Walnuts
Hindi	Amrud	Nimbu	Santra	Kishmish	Akhrot
Bengali	Payara	Lebu	Kamla lebu	Kishmish	Akhrot
Assamese	Madhurium	Nemu	Sumothira	Sukan angoor	Akhrot
Oriya	Piuli	Lembu	Kamala	Kismis	Akhrot
Marathi	Peru	Limbu	Santre	Bedane	Akrod
Gujarati	Jamrukh	Limbu	Santara	Lal draksh	Akhrot
Telugu	Jaamapandu	Nimma	Kamala Pandu	Kismis pallu	Aakrot
Kannada	Seebe	Nimbe	Kittale	Dweepadrakshi	Acrota
Tamil	Koyyapazham	Elumicham pazham	Kichilipazham	Ular dhraakshai	Akhrot
Malayalam	Perakkai	Cherunaranga	Madhura naranga	Unakkamunthiri	Akrotandi

Contd...

DRY SPICES

English	Aniseed	Asafoetida	Basil leaves	Bay leaf	Caraway seeds	Cardamom (brown)	Cardamom (green)	Cinnamon
Hindi	Saunf	Hing	Tulse ke patte	Tej patta	Shahjeera	Moti elaichi	Choti elaichi	Dalchini
Bengali	Mowri	Hing	Tulsi pata	Tej pata	Sajeera	Elach (tamate)	Elach (sobooj)	Daroochini
Assamese	Guwamori	Hing	Tulosi paat	Tejpaat	Bilati jira	Ilachi (muga)	Ilachi (sevjia)	Dalcheni
Oriya	Panamahuri	Hengu	Tulasi patra	Teja patra	Sahajira	Aleicha	Gijuratie	Dalachini
Marathi	Badishep	Hing	Tulsichi paney	Tamal patra	Shahjeera	Masala welchi	Welchi (hirvi)	Dalchini
Gujarati	Variyali	Hing	Tulsina pan	Tamal patra	Jiru	Etcho	Lila alchi	Tuj
Telugu	Sopagnja	Inguva	Thulasi akulu	—	Seema sopygrinjale	Yalakulu	Yala kulu (pachavi)	Dalchina chekka
Kannada	Sopubeeja	Hingu	Tulasi ele	—	Caraway beejagalre	Yalakki	Yalakki (hasuru)	Dalchini
Tamil	Perumjeerakam	Perungaayam	Thulasi	—	Karunjeerakam	Elakkai (Pazhuppu)	Elakkai (pachchai)	Lavangapattai
Malayalam	Perumjeerakam	Kaayam	Tulasi	—	Karunjeerakam	Elakkaya	Pach Elakkaya	Karuvapatta
Kashmiri	—	Yangu	—	—	—	Aal budu'a aal	—	—

Contd...

English	Cloves	Coriander seeds	Cumin seeds	Fenugreek seeds	Mace	Mustard seeds	Nutmeg	Parsley
Hindi	Laung	Sukha dhania	Jeera	Methi dana	Javitri	Rai	Jaiphal	Ajmooda ka patta
Bengali	Labango	Dhonay	Jeera	Methi	Jaeetri	Sarsay	Jaifall	Parsley
Assamese	Long	Dhania guti	Gota jeera	Paleng	Janee	Sarioh guti	Jaaiphal	Sugandhi lota
Oriya	Labanga	Dhania	Jira	Methi	Jayatree	Sorisha	Jaiphala	Balabalua shaga
Marathi	Lavanga	Dhane	Jire	Methi dane	Jaypatri	Mohari	Jayphal	Ajmoda
Gujarati	Laving	Dhana	Jeeru	Methi	Jaypatra	Rai	Jaypal	Ajmo
Telugu	Lavangalu	Dhaniyalu	Jeelakara	Menthulu	Japathri	Aavaalu	Jaikaaya	Kothimeerajati koora
Kannada	Lavanga	Kottambari beeja	Jeerige	Menthe	Japatri	Sasive kalu	Jaika	Kottambari jotiya soppu
Tamil	Kraambu	Koththamali virai	Jeerakam	Vendhayam	Jaadipathri	Kadugu	Jaadhikai	Kothamalu ilaigal pole
Malayalam	Karayaamboovu	Kothamalli	Jeerakam	Uluva	Jathipathri	Kadugu	Jathikka	Malliela pole
Kashmiri	Ru'ang	Daaniwal	Zyur	—	Jalwatur	—	Zaaphal	—

53

English	Peppercorns	Pomegranate seeds	Poppy seeds	Red Chillies	Tamarind	Turmeric	Vinegar	Thymol
Hindi	Kali mirch ke daane	Anardana	Khus khus	Lal mirch	Imli	Haldi	Sirka	Ajwain
Bengali	Marich	Dareem bij	Posto	Paka lonka	Tentool	Halood	Seerka	–
Assamese	Jaluk	Dalim guti	–	Sukan jalakia	Teteli	Halodhi	Sirika	–
Oriya	Golamaricha	Dalimba manji	–	Nali lankamaricha	Tentuli	Haladi	Vinegar	–
Marathi	Kale Miri	Dalimbache dane	Khas khas	Lal mirchya	Chincha	Halad	Sirka	Onva
Gujarati	Mari	Dadamna bee	Khaskhas	Lal marcha	Amli	Haldar	Sirko	–
Telugu	Miriyaalu	Daanimma ginjalu	Gasagasaalu	Erra mirapa kayalu	Chinthapandu	Pasupu	–	–
Kannada	Menasina kalu	Dalimbo beeja	Gasagase beeja	Kempu menasinakai	Hunase hannu	Arasina	–	–
Tamil	Milagu	Maadhulai vidhai	Kasakasaa	Milagai vatal	Puli	Manjal	Pulikaadi	–
Malayalam	Kurumulagu	Madhala naranga kuru	Kaskas	Chuvanna Mulagu	Puli	Manjal	Vinagiri	–

Also Available in Hindi

Also Available in Hindi

Also Available in Kannada, Tamil

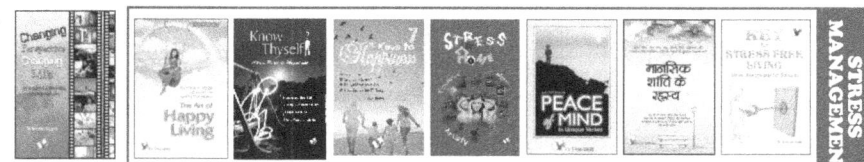

Also Available in Kannada

Also Available in Kannada

All books available at www.vspublishers.com

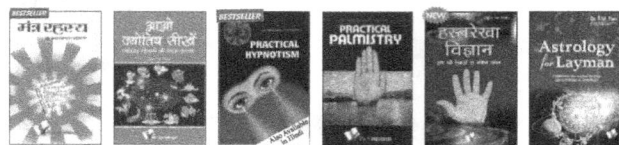

Also Available in Hindi, Kannada

Also Available in Hindi, Kannada